Guided Meditations for Children 2

How to Teach Children to Pray Using Scripture

Jane Reehorst, B.V.M.

BROWN ROA
Publishing Media

ISBN 0–697–02988–3

10 9 8 7 6 5 4

Table of Contents

Foreword: *Teaching Children to Pray Using
    Scripture*   v

Meditations

1. The Annunciation: *Faith and Trust in God*   1
2. The Visitation: *Sharing the Good News about
    Jesus*   5
3. The Birth of Jesus: *Welcoming Jesus into
    Your Life*   9
4. Finding Jesus in the Temple: *Obedience*   13
5. Call of the First Disciples: *Called to Know
    Jesus*   17
6. Jesus Blesses the Children: *Trusting God—
    The Joy of Being a Friend of Jesus*   21
7. Jesus Calms the Storm: *"Why Are You
    Afraid?"—Trusting*   25
8. Parable of the Talents: *Using Our Talents*   29
9. The Lost Sheep: *Forgiveness*   33
10. The Prodigal Son: *God Forgives Us*   37
11. The Good Samaritan: *Who Is Our Neighbor?*   41
12. The Rich Young Man: *Sharing with Others*   45
13. The Wicked Servant: *Forgiving Others*   49
14. Mary and Martha: *Friendship*   55
15. Jesus Washes the Feet of His Disciples:
    Helping Others   59
16. The Last Supper: *Jesus' Love for Us*   63
17. The Vine and Branches: *We Need Jesus as
    Our Friend, Jesus Wants to be Our Best Friend*   67
18. Peter Denies He Knows Jesus: *Honesty and
    Faithfulness*   73
19. Jesus Carries His Cross: *Loving Your Neighbor*   77
20. Easter Morning: *Celebrate! Jesus has Risen!*   81
21. On the Road to Emmaus: *Keeping a Promise*   85

Indexes

A. Biblical Passages   88
B. Human Experience Symbols   89
C. Gospel Images   90

Foreword:
Teaching Children to
Pray Using Scripture

These meditations were written for parents and teachers of children in the primary grades. The book shares a simple process which teaches children **how** to pray through meditation on the Scriptures. This process leads children into the Scripture scene where they meet Jesus personally and are encouraged to talk, and listen, to Him—which is prayer.

Since these particular meditations were written for children in the primary grades, they have been shortened and scholarly details have been omitted. Children at this age are open, uncomplicated, and direct. They are highly imaginative and, therefore, become quickly involved in the gospel scene simply presented as it is.

You will note that questions are often inserted into the meditations. This approach not only allows children to *quietly* express their feelings and more fully participate in the gospel scene, it also addresses the problem of their limited attention span.

The parables are simply worded and referred to as "stories which Jesus tells." Children will love to listen to these parables because they love stories, and because they are personally invited by Jesus to come, sit beside Him, and listen to His story!

Each meditation closes with Jesus addressing a question or a statement to the child personally. The question-statement focuses on the lesson He is teaching, and is a "conversation starter" with Him. Therefore, this part of the meditation is the "key" in teaching children what it means to pray and to have a personal relationship with Jesus, their friend. This "silent time" should be no longer than one minute.

Suggestions

1. Prior to presenting a meditation, allow yourself time to personally reflect on the gospel scene so you become comfortable with this prayer form.

2. Create an atmosphere of prayer . . . gentle discipline if necessary . . . possibly some soft background music. Make this the children's *special time with Jesus.*

3. Allow children to choose a comfortable position.

4. Read slowly, with slight pauses where indicated.

5. Participate in the meditation as you present it to the children.

6. Invite the children to pray spontaneously after your closing prayer. This will not be a problem for the primary grades.

7. After personal reflection on a particular gospel scene, do not hesitate to tailor the meditation to better suit the needs of your children.

Teaching children how to come to the Lord will not only affect you and your class now, it will also lead children into a life-long habit of effective prayer—and this is the heart of religious education.

The Annunciation

Luke 1:26–38

Faith and Trust in God

Introduction

Do you believe what your mother or father tells you? Do you believe what your teacher tells you? When your teacher tells you that it is important to learn how to read, do you believe your teacher? Why do you believe? (Allow for a few minutes discussion.) You have confidence and trust that what they tell you is the truth. In other words, you have *faith* in your parents and teachers. Faith also is believing in God and in what Jesus told us, even though we have never seen Jesus or God.

Jesus' mother, Mary, had great faith. She trusted God when God sent His angel to her to tell her she was going to have a baby. Let's go to Mary's house and be with her when the angel comes, shall we?

Close your eyes. . . . Take a deep breath . . . and relax. . .

Meditation

You are outside of Mary's house. . . . It is early morning and the sun has colored the sky all orange. . . . The birds must be happy about this. . . . Listen to them sing! . . . Open the door to Mary's house and walk in. . . . It's all right, because I think she is expecting you. . . . Do you see that door just ahead of you? . . . That's the door to Mary's bedroom. . . . Walk over to the door. . . . It's slightly open. . . . Quietly walk in. . . .

See, Mary is praying. . . . She sees you and welcomes you with a smile. . . . She calls you by name and invites you to sit down next to her. . . . Walk over and sit next to Mary. . . . It feels good to be with Mary, doesn't it?

A bright light fills the room. . . . Look! There is a beautiful angel standing in the middle of the light. . . . Mary smiles at the angel . . . and the angel says "Hello Mary" and turns to you and says hello to you! . . . Feel your heart pound. . . . Listen, the angel is saying something to Mary. . . . He is telling her not to be afraid and that God sent him to tell her that she is going to have a baby and she should name the baby, Jesus. . . . "Will you be Jesus' mother?" the angel asks. . . . Mary is smiling and nodding her head . . . and tells the angel . . . "I don't understand, but whatever God wants me to do I will do, because I trust God . . . so, yes, angel, I will be Jesus' mother."

The angel smiles at Mary and disappears. . . . Mary looks at you, takes your hand . . . and both of you look at the place where the angel was. . . . Then Mary turns to you and asks, "Do you think it is important to trust God?"

I will give you a little time to talk with Mary about trusting in God. (Allow a half minute or until there is a hint of restlessness . . . about a minute.)

Prayer

Mary, I'm glad you said "yes" to the angel and are Jesus' mother. I would like to be your friend so that you can help me trust God like you do. And please teach me all about Jesus, because you are his mother and know all about him. I love you, Mary. Amen.

It is time to leave Mary. . . . Say good-bye. . . . Get up and go to the door. . . . Turn and smile and wave good-bye. . . . Go through the door. . . . Open your eyes and come back into the room.

Sharing

When someone says, "I trust you," what does that mean to you? How would you show a friend that you trusted him or her? What did Mary do to show she trusted God? What can people your age do to show that they trust God?

Follow-up

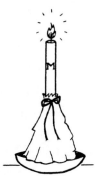

Show the children how to fashion a "Mary Candle." Midway around a tall, white candle, wrap material in skirt-like fashion. Use blue ribbon to hold the material in place, and tie a bow in front. Explain that the pure wax candle represents Mary, who is without sin. She holds within her—like the wick inside the candle—Jesus, the Light of the world.

If time allows, have the children decorate their own candles. Have the children wrap a small piece of material in skirt-like fashion midway around the candle. Give them a blue ribbon to tie the material in place. The letters "M" and "J" can be cut from foil or paper and glued to the candle, front and back.

Closing Prayer

Call the children together around the Mary Candle. Light the candle. Pray together "the Hail Mary," or a decade of the rosary.

Music

"Hail, Mary: Gentle Woman" by Carey Landry from *Glory and Praise* 1 (NALR)

"Speak, Lord." by the Dameans from *Glory and Praise* 2 (NALR)

"Sing of Mary" (traditional melody)

The Visitation

Luke 1:39–56

Sharing the Good News about Jesus

Introduction

Have you ever had something wonderful happen to you or to someone in your family? Maybe you got a new puppy or one of your parents got a new job or you went some place very special. (Allow time for sharing.) What were we just doing? That's right. We were sharing some of your good news with each other. When you first receive good news is there anyone special with whom you like to share it?

The Blessed Mother, Mary, received some wonderful news from a very special person. Do you know what her good news was? Who was the special person who told her? Mary wanted to share her wonderful news with someone special—just like we do—so she went to her favorite cousin, Elizabeth. Let's be with Mary and her cousin Elizabeth when this happens, shall we? Close your eyes. . . . Take a deep breath . . . and relax. . . .

Meditation

You and Mary's cousin, Elizabeth, are standing by Elizabeth's garden gate waiting for Mary to come visit you. . . . The path is a dirt path, not like the sidewalks that we have today. . . . It's a very nice day. . . . The blue sky has only three puffy white clouds. . . . Do you see them? . . . Feel the cool breeze on your face . . .

and, if you turn around, you can see Elizabeth's yard . . . and the beautiful red and yellow flowers under the tree. . . . Don't they smell wonderful? . . . Even the birds must be happy in this beautiful garden. . . . Listen to their songs! . . . There's a table in the shade of the tree and, on the table, there is a plate of delicious cookies and a pitcher of juice. . . . Don't take any now. . . . Let's wait for Mary to come. . . .

Elizabeth's dog is barking. . . . Look, he is running down the path and wagging his tail. . . . He's greeting someone. . . . It must be Mary. . . . It is! . . . Run and greet her! . . . Mary recognizes you, smiles, and calls you by name. . . . She is glad to see you, isn't she? . . . Are you glad to see Mary? . . . She's very pretty, isn't she? . . . Take Mary's hand and walk with her to Elizabeth who is now walking down the path toward you. . . . The three of you . . . And the dog, of course, . . . Walk into the garden. . . . Mary stops . . . puts one hand on your shoulder and one hand on Elizabeth's shoulder. . . . Her eyes are shining . . . and there are happy tears in them. She can't wait to tell you something. . . . "God has done a wonderful thing to me . . . of all people!" she tells you . . . she looks directly into your eyes, and almost whispers, "I am going to be the mother of Jesus! Feel your heart pound with excitement at this wonderful news! Mary's hand gently squeezes your shoulder. . . . "Isn't God wonderful!" she says. . . . Elizabeth hugs both of you. . . . She is very excited. . . . "I knew! I knew God had blessed you in some special way just as soon as I saw your face!" she exclaims. . . . Mary looks at Elizabeth . . . smiles . . . now she looks at you and asks, "What do you think of my wonderful news?" . . . What would you like to say to Mary? I'll give you a quiet time so that you can share with Mary her good news.

Prayer

Mary, I am so happy to be with you and share your wonderful news. . . . God is so good to us . . . to give us His only Son, Jesus. I want to celebrate with you . . . and I want to go out and tell everyone I know the Good News. . . . Thank you, Mary, for sharing with me.

... I'm glad you are Jesus' mother. . . . And I love you. Amen.

It is time to leave Mary and Elizabeth. . . . Say good-bye. . . . Turn and begin to walk out of the garden. . . . Stop and turn and wave good-bye once more. . . . Walk out of the garden. . . . Open your eyes and come back into the room.

Sharing

Who was Elizabeth? Why did Mary go to visit her? What good news did Mary have to tell Elizabeth? What did Elizabeth say to Mary when she heard Mary's good news?

Follow-up

Have the children design a "good news" banner. Have cut beforehand the following number of these capital letters: E (7), V (1), R (2), Y (1), O (4), N (2), H (2), A (3), S (3), P (1), I (2), C (1), F (1), G (1), D (1), W (1), T (1).

Randomly distribute the letters equally among the children. Tell the children that they are free to decorate the letters in whatever style they choose, using magic markers. When the children have finished decorating their letters, arrange the letters on a large poster board, so that they read:

"Everyone has a piece of good news. Share it!"

Point out to the children that the sign is beautiful and colorful because it represents a piece of all of them.

Closing Prayer

Pray with the children Mary's prayer of praise, the Magnificat by reading the prayer to the children, using either a children's Bible or the Good News Bible. Have the children echo the prayer, line by line, after you.

Music

"My Soul Magnifies the Lord" by Carey Landry from *Hi God!* 2 (NALR)

"My Soul Rejoices" by the Dameans from *Glory and Praise* 3 (NALR)

"I Am a Servant" by Lorraine Louvat from *I Could Have Been a Bumblebee* (BROWN Publishing–ROA Media)

The Birth of Jesus

Luke 2:8–20

Welcoming Jesus into Your Life

Introduction

Have you ever had someone you liked very much come to your house to visit you? How did you welcome or greet this person? In what way did that person respond to your welcome? How does it feel to be welcomed, to have someone be glad to see you? Do you suppose Mary and Joseph felt happy to see the shepherds come to welcome their new-born baby, Jesus? Let's be with the shepherds that wonderful night when Jesus was born. Would you like that? Close your eyes. . . . Take a deep breath . . . and relax. . . .

Meditation

It is night time. . . . You are with the shepherds helping them keep watch over the sheep, protecting them from harm. . . . Walk over to the fence where the sheep are kept. . . . Listen to them "baa" . . . I suppose that is the sheep saying "good night" to each other. . . . Look at the baby sheep, called lambs. Aren't they tiny and cute? We better let them sleep for now. . . . The shepherds are sitting by a fire. . . . Walk over to them. . . . They welcome you and invite you to sit by the fire with them. . . . The night is a little cool, so it feels good to sit by the warm fire, doesn't it? . . . A shepherd touches your shoulder and points to a bright star in the sky. . . . "We've never seen that star before. . . . It's a new star," he tells you. . . .

Look! The sky is suddenly very bright!...And...and...there is an angel...a beautiful angel right here before you!... Listen, the angel is saying something....

"Don't be afraid, I come to bring you good news. ...Jesus the Savior was born today!... You will find him with his mother and father in a manger-cave just outside of Bethlehem."

Look! There are more angels!... They are singing because they are so happy.... Listen to their song....

"Glory to God in the highest! And on earth peace to those with whom His favor rests!"

The angels are gone now... and, for a minute, all of you just sit in silence.... One of the shepherds gets up and says... "Let's hurry and go to Bethlehem and welcome Jesus."... Another shepherd asks all of you, "What gift can we bring to Jesus?"... Run over and pick up one of the little lambs you saw earlier.... Feel how soft it is!... It cuddles up to you.... Tell the shepherds that you will give Jesus this lamb.... They are all happy about your suggestion, aren't they?... All of you hurry toward the cave.... See that bright star?... It is shining right over the cave.... Stand by the entrance to the cave.... See Mary and Joseph? ... Mary is holding a baby.... It is Jesus!... Joseph sees you... smiles and invites you into the cave.... Walk up to Mary.... Kneel down and place your tiny lamb on the straw in front of Jesus.... Mary and Joseph smile at you.... Joseph pets the lamb and thanks you.... "Would you like to hold Jesus?" Mary asks you.... Hold out your arms and let Mary place Jesus into your arms.... How does it feel to hold the baby Jesus in your arms? What would you like to say to Jesus? I will give you a quiet time now so that you can talk to Jesus....

Prayer

Jesus, thank you for coming to us. I am glad I am here with you because I can tell you that I love you and welcome you into this world. I want you to be my best friend. I love you very much, Jesus. Amen.

It is time to leave. . . . Give Jesus back to Mary. . . . Say good-bye to Jesus . . . Mary . . . and Joseph. . . . Get up and walk out of the cave. . . . Turn and wave good-bye once more. . . . Open your eyes and come back into the room.

Sharing

Think of Christmas. Whose birthday do we celebrate? Who are some of the people who prepared to see Mary, Joseph, and Jesus on that first Christmas? How can we prepare to celebrate Jesus' birthday?

Follow-up

Show the children how to make a wreath. Use paper plates with the center cut out before time.

Give the children green tissue-paper squares. Instruct the children to put a drop of white glue or paste on the circle and cover with a tissue paper square, pinching up the sides of the tissue square. Do this again and again until the ring is covered.

Fold red construction paper in half, widthwise, and cut out a red bow and some berries. Glue or paste onto wreath. Explain that the wreath represents a welcome sign. It can be hung on a door or anywhere in the home to show others that you welcome them. Our wreath is a reminder of how we can welcome Jesus on Christmas by praying and doing good actions.

Variation: Torn paper can be used instead of tissue. In this case, the children tear small pieces of paper and cover the wreath in mosaic fashion.

Closing Prayer

Gather the children near the Bible and candle. Pray: Each year we prepare to celebrate God's special gift, Jesus. Pick up the Bible and say, "God so loved the world, that He gave His only Son." (John 3:16)

Now let us welcome Jesus into our hearts and homes. Let us pray for us. (Each child says his or her

wreath

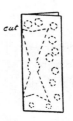

cut

bow and berries

name aloud. If there are many children, they whisper names together.)

Invite all to raise hands in gesture of blessing:

We praise You, Lord Jesus. (hands above head)

Bless each one of *us*. (hands on chest)

We welcome You into our *hearts*. (hands folded in prayer)

Music

"Come, Lord Jesus" by Carey Landry from *Hi God! 2* or *Young People's Glory and Praise* (NALR)

"O Come, O Come, Emmanuel" first verse and refrain (traditional)

Finding Jesus in the Temple

Luke 2:41–52

Obedience

Introduction

Sometimes it is hard to obey, isn't it? Have you ever been with a friend having a good time playing your favorite game and your friend was called to supper? How did you feel about this? How did your friend react? Was it hard to obey when you were having such a good time? Or, have you ever forgotten to tell your parents that you'd be at a friend's house? What happened? Were they worried?

This happened to Mary and Joseph. They lost Jesus for three whole days. Isn't that terrible? How do you think they felt? You see, they were on their way home from the big Passover celebration in Jerusalem when they discovered that Jesus was not with them. Joseph thought Jesus was with Mary, and Mary thought He was with Joseph. So they hurried back to Jerusalem as fast as they could and looked all over for him. Finally, they decided to look in the Temple. Let's be with Mary and Joseph when they go to the Temple to look for Jesus, shall we? Close your eyes. . . . Take a deep breath . . . and relax. . . .

Meditation

You are with Mary and Joseph entering the Temple courtyard. . . . Look at all the tall white pillars! . . . They are so tall they make you feel like a tiny ant, don't they? . . . It is nice and cool in here, isn't it? . . . Look

13

around and see all the people. . . . Some are just standing by themselves thinking . . . and others are visiting with each other. . . . Joseph walks over to a man. . . . He is asking if he saw Jesus. . . . Look! The man is nodding "yes.". . . He's pointing to the other side of the courtyard. . . . Mary rests her hand on your shoulder and whispers, "I think we have found Jesus." . . . Joseph hurries over to you and Mary . . . looks at Mary and nods his head and smiles. . . . "Come," is all he says. . . . Take Mary and Joseph's hands and let them lead you to Jesus.

Joseph stops . . . points toward a group of important teachers sitting together. . . . "There he is," he whispers to Mary and you. . . . Mary sighs, leans against Joseph, and whispers, "We have found our son." . . . Joseph places his hand on your shoulder and says, "Quietly go over and tell Jesus to come here. . . . Try not to disturb the others." . . . Start walking toward Jesus. . . . Don't run . . . walk slowly. . . . Jesus sees you and smiles. . . . Point toward Mary and Joseph and beckon Jesus to come. . . . Jesus nods his head . . . gets up, and follows you. . . .

Mary walks up to Jesus. . . . She looks very serious, doesn't she? . . . "My child," she says to Jesus, "why have you done this to us? See how worried your father and I have been looking for you?" . . . Mary waits for Jesus to explain himself. . . . "I'm sorry I made you worry," Jesus says, "but didn't you know that I must begin to do what my Father in heaven told me to do?" Joseph and Mary look at each other puzzled. . . . Joseph shakes his head . . . places his hands on Jesus' shoulders and looks into his eyes. . . . "Jesus, you are never to do this to us again. . . . We are still your parents and you must obey us. . . . Do you understand this?" . . . Jesus nods his head. . . . There are tears in his eyes as he says, "Please forgive me for causing you so much worry." Joseph nods his head . . . turns and says, "Come, it's getting late." You and Jesus follow Mary and Joseph out of the Temple.

Jesus looks at you. He knows you are his friend and will be truthful with him. . . . "I've caused all of you much worry, haven't I?" Jesus asks. . . . He looks at

Mary and Joseph walking ahead and sighs. . . . "I love my parents and never want to hurt them. . . . I feel sad about what I have done." . . . Jesus turns to you and asks, "Has this ever happened to you? . . . How did it make you feel?" I will give you a quiet time so that you and Jesus can talk about this.

Prayer

Jesus, sometimes I have hurt my parents, too . . . making them worry about me. . . . I know you understand because this happened to you. When I am tempted to disobey, be with me and help me. I know you will, Jesus, because you are my friend. Amen.

It is time to leave. . . . Say good-bye to Jesus, Mary, and Joseph and begin to walk away. . . . Turn and wave good-bye once more. . . . Continue to walk away. . . . Open your eyes and come back into the room.

Sharing

Who was lost? How did Mary and Joseph feel? Where did they find Jesus? When Mary asked Jesus to explain what happened, what did He say? When we disobey or worry those who care for us, what should we say? How do we show we are really sorry?

Follow-up

Beforehand have ready 7" diameter circles, cut from tagboard or light-colored construction paper.

Give each child a circle. Instruct the children to make a self-portrait depicting a happy face. Children can color in or paste with torn paper their hair, eyes, mouth, and so on. Explain that when we are lost and then found, or had a quarrel and made up, we feel happy to be together again.

Closing Prayer

Gather in a semi-circle around the Bible and candle. Then invite the children to pray, "I am sorry, dear Jesus, for all the times I have failed to love." (Pause.) "Thank You, dear Jesus, for being my best friend, for always loving me. Help me to keep close to You always. Bless all who care for me. Give me peace and joy. Give others peace and joy, also. Make us happy followers of You."

Close with a familiar song or one of the suggested songs.

Music

"Oh, How I Love Jesus!" by Carey Landry, from *Hi God!* (NALR)

"Joy, Joy, Joy" by Carey Landry from *Hi God!* (NALR)

Call of the First Disciples

Matthew 4:18–22; Mark 1:16–20

Called to Know Jesus

Introduction

Do you love Jesus? Do you like to talk to Jesus? What do you think are some things children would tell Jesus? Do you know what it means to be a special friend? Do special friends like to be with each other? Do you follow your special friend when he wants you to go with him some place? Why? Jesus had just made some new special friends and he wanted them to be with him. Wouldn't it be nice to have Jesus as your special friend and to be with him whenever you wanted to? Let's go and be with Jesus at this time as he is gathering his special friends. . . . Close your eyes. . . . Take a deep breath . . . and relax. . . .

Meditation

You are standing on the beach by the Sea of Galilee, waiting for Jesus. . . . Right by the water there are some fishermen sitting near their boats cleaning their nets . . . getting them ready for the next time they go out. . . . Do you see them? . . . There is a smell of fish in the air. . . . It doesn't smell too nice, does it? . . . I guess those fishermen are used to the smell, don't you suppose? . . . Look at the sky! . . . It's all oranges, reds, and yellows from the sun just beginning to rise. . . . Isn't it beautiful? . . . Dig your feet into the cool sand and let the sand squish between your toes. . . . That's fun, isn't it?

17

Look up the beach. . . . Jesus is coming! . . . He is walking toward you. . . . Run and meet him. . . . Jesus sees you . . . stops . . . calls out your name and opens his arms. . . . Run into his arms. . . . Doesn't it feel good to be hugged by Jesus? . . . I'm happy you have come," Jesus tells you. . . . "I'm going to see if those four fishermen will come with me and be my special friends." . . . Jesus walks up to the first boat and asks Peter and Andrew to come with him. . . . They look surprised, don't they? . . . But look! They put down their nets and come with Jesus. . . . Jesus goes up to James and John and invites them to follow him. . . . They nod excitedly and get up and follow Jesus. . . .

Jesus sees that you might be surprised. . . . "Peter," Jesus says, "why don't you explain to my friend here why you just dropped everything to come with me." . . . Peter looks at you . . . smiles to himself . . . shakes his head . . . shrugs his shoulders and says, "I really don't know why. . . . All I know is that once I got to know Jesus, I wanted to be with him." . . . The other apostles nod and agree. . . . Jesus smiles at them . . . looks at you . . . places his hand on your shoulder and asks. . . . "Would you like me to be your special friend?" . . . What would you like to say to Jesus? . . . Walk with Jesus to the edge of the water and sit down with him. . . . I'll give you some quiet time so that the two of you can talk together.

Prayer

Jesus, it's good to be here on the beach with you. I want so much to have you as my very special friend. . . . We can share secrets together like special friends do. . . . And it is so good to know that you will always be with me. I love you, Jesus, my special friend. Amen.

It is time to leave Jesus. . . . Walk down the beach a little way with Jesus. . . . Now begin to walk away. . . . Turn around and wave good-bye to your friend once more. . . . Open your eyes and come back into the room.

Sharing

Can you name the fishermen that Jesus called to be His first friends? What did they do when He called them to be His friends? Does Jesus want to be your special friend? How can you speak to Jesus and be close to Jesus always? How can you show Jesus that you love Him?

Follow-up

Instruct the children to cut out a heart, as follows.

Fold a (9" x 12") piece of red construction paper in half in either direction and cut out half a heart, then open it out to a whole heart. A simple way is to place the thumb on the fold and cut around the edge.

Children print on the front of the heart, "Jesus is My Friend." On the back of the heart, they print

"Love, from _____." The children may add
              (name)
decorations to their hearts.

Punch hole in top and loop yarn or string through. Fasten, and invite the children to hang their heart in a favorite place as a reminder of Jesus' friendship with them.

Closing Prayer

Call the children together around the Bible and candle. Say, "Jesus speaks to us in God's special Book. Jesus says, 'I am God and I call you by name.' " Take each child's hands in yours and say

"N _____, Jesus is your friend." Close by praying the Sign of the Cross together.

Music

"Come Along with Me to Jesus" by Carey Landry from *Hi God! 2* (NALR)

"Yes, Lord, Yes" by Carey Landry from *Hi God! 2* (NALR)

Jesus Blesses the Children

Mark 10:13–16; Matthew 19:13–15;
Luke 18:15–17

Trusting God
The Joy of Being a Friend of Jesus

Introduction

Do you know someone whom you love to be with? How do you feel when you are told that that person is coming to your house for a visit? Why do you like that person so much? Do you trust that person? Why?

I know a person who not only enjoys being with you but who also loves you very much. And you can always trust that person. Do you know who that person is? Yes, it is Jesus. Shall we go and visit Jesus? Close your eyes. . . . Take a deep breath . . . and relax. . . .

Meditation

You are in a lovely field. . . . There are many beautiful trees that you can climb . . . or just sit under, in their cool shade. . . . Do you see the yellow and blue wildflowers all over the field? . . . Isn't it a beautiful field? . . . Listen to all the songs of the birds. . . . Do you see them perched on the tree branches? . . . And look at all the butterflies dancing from flower to flower! . . . It's just a wonderful day to be in this lovely field, isn't it? . . . There are also many children running and playing tag in the field. . . . Hear them laugh and shout? . . . Would you like to play with them? . . . Wait! . . . Someone is calling your name. . . . Look . . . over there, under the tree just ahead of you, where all the

21

grown ups are sitting!... It's Jesus who is calling you!... Run over to him!... Jesus invites you to sit on his lap.... Doesn't it feel good to be so close to Jesus?

All of the other children are also coming to be with Jesus.... They are laughing and talking and seem to be just as happy as you are to be here with Jesus.... And look!... Jesus is laughing too and enjoying having all of you close to him.... Some of Jesus' disciples are trying to make you children be quiet and leave Jesus... but Jesus is enjoying all of these happy, laughing children.... He turns to the disciples and tells them to let you all stay with Him.... "See how these children enjoy life!... They do not worry."... Jesus lays his cheek on top of your head, smiles, and says to the grown-ups... "They trust their heavenly Father, for they know their heavenly Father loves them and protects them."... Jesus looks at you and says, "I'm glad you trust me and are not afraid to come to me and just be with me.... I know you are my friend.... This is what the Kingdom of Heaven is all about."

Would you like to tell Jesus that you love and trust him? I'll give you some quiet time so that you can talk, and listen, to Jesus.

Prayer

Jesus, I'm glad you are my friend and that you're always here waiting for me to come to you... because, Jesus, I can share my secrets with you.... I trust you. And I love you very much. Amen.

It's time to leave Jesus. Say good-bye.... Begin to walk away.... Turn and wave good-bye to Jesus.... Continue to walk away.... Open your eyes and come back into the room.

Sharing

Do you think Jesus showed how He loved children? Jesus said that the Kingdom of Heaven is like children who love and trust. How can we show our love and trust for Jesus?

Follow-up

Pass out (12" x 24") pieces of construction paper. Have the directions printed on the board or poster, or give oral directions to guide the children.

Draw a lovely field.

Draw a tree and make Jesus under the tree.

Make children playing.

Make you close to Jesus.

Make men in the field.

Draw yellow and blue flowers.

Draw birds in the sky.

Draw a sun in the sky.

Have the children turn the paper over and print, "Jesus Blesses the Children." Then sign their name. Allow time to have some of the children retell the story in their own words.

Closing Prayer

Jesus loves us. Jesus wants us to come to Him. We share every time we pray. Let's hold hands and pray the prayer Jesus gave us, the "Our Father." Then the leader or parent, raises hands in blessing: "May God, the Father, the Son, and Holy Spirit bless you and keep you in His love always." Amen."

Music

"The Lord's Prayer" by Eric Sylvester from *Glory & Praise 1* (NALR)

"Sing a Simple Song" by Carey Landry from *Hi God 2* (NALR)

Jesus Calms the Storm

Mark 4:35–42; Luke 8:22–25;
Matthew 8:23–27

"Why Are You Afraid?"
Trusting

Introduction

Have you ever been afraid? What do you do when you are afraid? Do you go to someone you trust for safety? Do you want to talk to that person about your fears? What does this person tell you? How do you feel after you are with this person? There was one special time when the apostles were very much afraid. I wonder how they handled their fear. Let's be with them and find out, shall we?

Close your eyes. . . . Take a deep breath . . . and relax. . . .

Meditation

You and the apostles are on a boat with Jesus. . . . You are on the Sea of Galilee, taking Jesus to the other side so that he can escape the crowds and rest. . . . He has been very tired lately. . . . The boat belongs to Peter. . . . It is a very large fishing boat. . . . Smell the sea air. . . . Take a deep breath and enjoy the cool air in your nose and lungs. . . . Put your hand in the water and feel how refreshing and cool the sea is. . . . And watch the seagulls swoop over the water. . . . They are looking for fish to eat. . . . Aren't they beautiful and graceful as they glide and swoop down toward the water?

The apostles are busy rowing the fishing boat. . . . They have to be very strong to row this large boat, don't they? . . . John whispers to you, "Jesus must be very tired; look, he is already asleep." Look toward the stern of the boat. (That's the back of the boat.) See Jesus lying fast asleep there on some pillows. . . . He looks so peaceful, doesn't he? . . . The once-gentle breeze now becomes stronger. Do you feel it? . . . Peter is looking up toward the sky. . . . He is frowning. . . . "It looks like a storm is coming up fast," he tells you. . . . The sea becomes rough . . . and large waves begin to rock the boat and fill it with water. . . . Are you afraid? . . . The apostles seem to be. . . . "Wake up, Jesus!" Peter yells. . . . You can hardly hear Peter because the sea is making so much noise. . . . John begins to crawl over to Jesus. . . . Crawl after John. Be careful. . . . He shakes Jesus' shoulder and yells. . . . "Jesus, save us or we will all drown!" . . .

Jesus wakes up. . . . He sits up and looks at the stormy sea . . . the water in the boat . . . and then at his disciples. . . . He raises his hands over the roaring sea and says, "Peace, be still." . . . Look! . . . The sea is calm . . . and the storm is gone! . . . Don't you feel relieved? . . . Jesus places his arm around your shoulders and says to you and the apostles, "Why are you afraid? Have you no faith?" . . . Watch the expression on the apostles' faces. . . . Their eyes are wide and their mouths are open. . . . First they look at Jesus, and then at the calm sea. . . . Peter looks again at Jesus and asks, "Who are you, Jesus, that even the wind and the sea obey you?" . . . Then he turns away and looks at the sea again. . . .

Jesus hugs you, smiles, and looks into your eyes. . . . "I understand when you are afraid," he tells you. . . . "And what I want you to do is to come to me when you are afraid, and tell me about your fears, even your smallest ones. . . . Will you allow me to help you? . . . Don't friends trust and help each other? . . . Jesus waits for your answer. . . .

I will give you a quiet time so that you can talk to Jesus and, if you have any fears, tell him about them.

Prayer

Jesus, I'm glad you calmed the storm.... Even though I don't have real sea storms in my life, there are other things that make me afraid.... I will come to you, Jesus, when I am afraid of something because you are my friend. You will help me. I trust you, Jesus. Amen.

It is time to leave Jesus.... Say good-bye.... Open your eyes and come back into the room.

Sharing

Would anyone want to share thoughts about being afraid? Why were Jesus and His apostles crossing the Sea of Galilee? Where was Jesus? What happened? What did Jesus say to the sea? What did Jesus say to the apostles? We can always know Jesus will help us when we are afraid.

Follow-up

Distribute (12" x 24") white construction paper. Give each child a (3" x 12") brown paper strip. Instruct the children to use the brown construction paper to cut

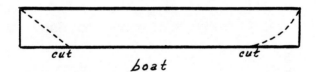

boat

"Peace"

out a boat. Cut off one end of the brown paper in diagonal fashion and round the other end, like a rowboat.

Paste the boat on the white construction paper. Allow children to draw in freely the water, the apostles, and Jesus blessing the sea.

Have small (2" x 3") multi-colored blank cards nearby. Allow the children to choose one and print on "Peace". They can paste the caption to their finished drawing.

Closing Prayer

Sit around the Bible and candle. Place the drawings by the Bible. The teacher prays:

"Jesus, teach us to ask others for help, especially when we feel afraid. Thank You, Jesus. We believe in Your love and care. Keep our family and friends safe from harm. Amen."

Sing a closing song.

Music

"Peace is Flowing Like a River" by Carey Landry from *Glory and Praise 1*—last verse (NALR)

"Great Things Happen!" by Carey Landry from *Glory and Praise 1*—third verse and refrain (NALR)

Parable of the Talents

Matthew 25:14–30; Luke 19:12–27

Using Our Talents

Introduction

All of us have talents, or abilities. Some seem to have more talents than others. . . . But we all have talents. Some people seem to be able to draw easily. They have a talent for drawing. Can you name talents that other people have? What are you good at, or what do you think your talent is? What happens if a person who is good at drawing never takes lessons or never draws? What about a football player who never trains or goes out for practice? Why do you suppose God gave us all different talents?

Jesus told a story about people using their talents. Let's go and listen to Jesus tell his story. . . . Close your eyes. . . . Take a deep breath . . . and relax. . . .

Meditation

You are in a field . . . and, if you look just ahead of you, you will see four or five shade trees. . . . There are people seated under one of the trees. . . . Walk over to the tree. . . . Someone calls your name. . . . It is Jesus. . . . "I've been waiting for you," Jesus tells you. . . . "I'm about to tell a story. . . . Come and sit next to me and listen to my story." . . . Hurry over and sit next to Jesus. . . . Are you comfortable? Good. . . . Jesus begins his story. . . .

"Once upon a time, a long time ago, there was a very rich man who was going to another country. He was going to be given a kingdom by the king of that country. Now the very rich man wanted the kingdom very much, but he also wanted to earn money while he was away. 'I have an idea,' he said to himself, 'I'll call all my servants together and instruct them to take the money I'll give them and to make more money for me.' And so the rich man did just that. To one servant, he gave a lot of money; to another, he did not give quite as much; and, to a third, he gave even less. To each he said, 'I have given you charge over my money; it is yours to invest and earn more money for me. Use it well.' And so the rich man left for another country.

"When he returned he called all his servants together and asked them to give an account of themselves. The first servant gave his master a large bag of money, saying, 'Here, master, I made ten times what you gave me.' The rich man was so pleased that he gave the servant charge over ten of his cities. The second servant gave his master a large bag of money and said, 'Look, master, I made five times what you gave me.' And the rich man was so happy that he gave this servant charge over five of his cities. Now when the third servant came before the master he said, 'Master, here is the amount of money you gave me. I hid it and did not use it because I was afraid that if I lost it you would punish me.' The rich man was so angry that he took the money away from the servant and gave it to the servant who had earned ten times the money for his master. Then the master warned all the servants, 'This wicked servant hid his money and did not use it. I gave him the money to use, not to hide. That is why I have taken it away and given it to the first servant who knows how to use the money I gave him.'"

Jesus finishes his story . . . turns to you . . . takes your hand . . . looks into your eyes . . . and asks, "Do you know that you were entrusted with very special talents by my Father just like the servants were entrusted with their master's money? What do you suppose you are to do with your talents?"

If you are not sure of your talents ask Jesus to help you know what they are. . . . I will give you a quiet time to talk to Jesus about your talents.

Prayer

Jesus, help me know what my talents are so that I can use them for you and share them with others. I don't want to be like the servant in your story who hid his talent. I want to make my talent better and better, just for you. Amen.

It is time to leave. . . . Thank Jesus for telling you his story. . . . Say good-bye. . . . Get up and begin to walk away. . . . Turn and wave to Jesus once more. . . . Walk away. . . . Open your eyes and come back into the room.

Sharing

What is a talent? Yes, it is an ability to do something. Why was the rich man pleased with the first two servants? Why was the rich man angry about the third? What do you suppose Jesus wants us to understand about using our abilities?

Follow-up

Invite the children to name all the talents they see in themselves and in others. Jot down responses on newsprint or blackboard, for example, drawing, baking, playing baseball, singing, writing, smiling, playing piano, and so on.

Instruct the children to make a Talent Mini-Banner.

Children choose multi-colored (12" x 24") construction paper and string or yarn.

Fold back the top of the banner. Line yarn or string under fold. Glue or staple down and then tie for hanging.

Explain to the children that they can make a talent banner by printing one of their talents or drawing a picture of themselves using a talent. Then decorate freely, and add their name on the right hand corner

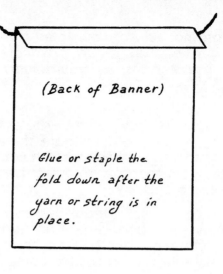

(Back of Banner)

Glue or staple the fold down after the yarn or string is in place.

of the banner. Encourage and assist when necessary, and comment on each child's talent.

Closing Prayer

Have the children place their talent mini-banner on a special table near the Bible and candle. Point over to the banners and say, "When we think of our talents we want to thank God for our gifts. We want to thank God for other people's talents, also."

Then teacher prays: "Thank You, Lord, for all these children and their precious talents."

(Invite the children to pray spontaneously in thanks.)

Pray the "Glory Be to the Father, and to the Son, and to the Holy Spirit. Amen." Conclude by singing a song.

Music

"Thank You, Lord" by Carey Landry from *Hi God! 1* (NALR)

"Celebrate God!" by Carey Landry from *Hi God! 1* (NALR)

The Lost Sheep

Luke 15:3–7; Matthew 18:1–14

Forgiveness

Introduction

Sometimes it is hard to be good, isn't it? How do you feel when you do something you know you are not supposed to do? Do you think you will be forgiven? Is it important for you to be forgiven?

Jesus wants to tell you a story about how much God loves you and wants to forgive you. Jesus wants to tell you this story also because he knows how important it is for you to know that you will *always* be forgiven by God.

So close your eyes.... Take a deep breath... and relax....

Meditation

You are in the country.... There are no houses or stores around.... Listen to the birds singing.... See that bird in the tree near you? ... It seems so happy singing, doesn't it? ... Do you see all the flowers... the blue ones... and even red ones? ... And look, there are sheep in the field! ... Do you see the tiny lamb by its mother? ... Go over and pet the lamb. ... Its wool is soft, isn't it? ... Someone is calling your name.... It is Jesus! ... He is sitting under that tree near the tiny lamb.... Run over to Jesus who is looking at you and smiling.... He pats the ground next to him.... "Come sit next to me," Jesus tells you.... "I want to tell you a story about my

Father's love for you."... Go over and sit next to Jesus and listen to his story.

"Once upon a time there was a shepherd taking care of his sheep ... just like that shepherd over there in the field walking with his sheep.... Do you see him? The shepherd loved his sheep very much ... and the sheep loved and trusted their shepherd for he protected them from wolves and others who would want to hurt them....

"One day as the shepherd was counting his sheep and putting them in a safe place for the night he noticed that one of his sheep was missing.... The shepherd ran over to the other shepherds who were also counting their sheep and putting them in the sheep pen for the night. 'Will you please watch my sheep?' he asked them, 'One of them is missing. It's that little rascal who is always wandering off ... getting into mischief.' The other shepherds shook their heads and said to each other, "Well, this time he's done it ... got himself lost.' They knew all about Fleetfoot. That was the name they had given the lost sheep, for he was always fleeing here and there, wandering away from the other sheep. 'Hope you find him before the wolves do.' they said. Fleetfoot's shepherd smiled sadly, turned, and hurried away ... calling Fleetfoot's name as he went. And when he heard the wolves howling, he called even louder....

"Suddenly he heard Fleetfoot calling out for help.... 'Baa ... baa,' cried the frightened Fleetfoot. ... 'I'm coming!' called the shepherd who saw Fleetfoot caught in a thorny bush. Gently the shepherd removed the branches of the thorny bush from Fleetfoot's wool ... lovingly picked him up ... and carried him back to the shepherds' camp. 'Look, I've found him!' he called out to the other shepherds.... 'Let's celebrate! Fleetfoot who was lost is now found!' All the shepherds had a party to celebrate Fleetfoot's return. And even though Fleetfoot had disobeyed, his shepherd was so happy to have him safely back with the other sheep that he happily forgave him."

Jesus turns to you ... hugs you ... and asks, "Do you see how much my Father loves you? ... Do you believe that my Father will forgive you, just as Fleet-foot was forgiven?"

(Allow about thirty seconds of silence—or longer, if the children seem to be relaxed.)

What would you like to tell Jesus? I'll give you time to talk to Jesus. . . .

Prayer

Jesus, sometimes I'm like Fleetfoot and do things I'm not supposed to do. . . . I'm so glad that you love me and forgive me. Thank you, Jesus, for taking care of me. I love you, Jesus. I'm glad you are my friend.

It's time to leave Jesus. . . . Say good-bye. . . . Get up and begin to walk away. . . . Turn and wave to Jesus. . . . Continue to walk away. . . . Open your eyes and come back into the room.

Sharing

Did the Good Shepherd forgive Fleetfoot for stray-ing? What did Jesus do? How did the others feel when Fleetfoot came back to the flock? Does Jesus ever stop loving or forgiving us?

Follow-up

Direct the children to make a "Good Shepherd" story booklet. Fold 9" x 12" paper to make four pages—front, back, and two inside pages. Number the pages 1, 2, 3, 4. Print directions on the board and go over them with the children.

Page 1 Make a flock of sheep.

Page 2 Make one sheep caught in a thorny bush.

Page 3 Make Jesus, the Good Shepherd, carrying the sheep home.

Page 4 Make all the sheep together again.
Print above the sheep, "Celebrate".

If time permits, allow the children to retell the story, looking at their pictures.

Closing Prayer

Gather the children close to the Bible and candle. Pick up the Bible reverently. Raise it high and announce its specialness. Lower the Bible and continue with:

"We hear of Jesus' goodness and love in the Gospel of John when Jesus says, "I am the Good Shepherd.

The Good Shepherd lays down His life for His sheep."

(John 10:11–15)

Call each child to you and personalize the message: "N _____, Jesus is the Good Shepherd who forgives you and cares for you."

Conclude the session with a simple Act of Contrition and/or sing a song.

Music

"Like a Shepherd" by Bob Dufford, S.J. (antiphon) from *Glory and Praise 1* (NALR)

"Psalm of the Good Shepherd" by Carey Landry from *Color the World with Song* (NALR)

"I Like God's Love" by Carey Landry from *Hi God!* (NALR)

The Prodigal Son

Luke 15:11–32

God Forgives Us

Introduction

Have you ever done anything for which you were sorry? Were you ever punished for this? After you were punished did you say you were sorry for what you did or said? When you were told that you were forgiven how did you feel?

Jesus was always telling people that his Father loved them so much that he was always waiting to forgive them. All they had to do was to come to him and be sorry. In fact, Jesus is about to tell a story to show how much his Father loves you and wants to forgive you. Shall we go to Jesus and listen to his story? . . . Close your eyes. . . . Take a deep breath . . . and relax. . . .

Meditation

You are standing by a stream. . . . Listen to its bubbly sound. . . . See how the water rolls over the little stones and turns white for a quick second when it hits the larger stones that stick up out of the water. . . . Put your hand in the water and feel how cool it is. . . .

Someone is calling your name. . . . Look! It is Jesus who is calling you. See, he is sitting under that tree just in front of you . . . the one by the stream. . . . He is inviting you to come and sit down next to him. . . . There are other children your age sitting with

Jesus. . . . Walk over to Jesus and sit next to him. . . . They are glad you joined them. . . . Jesus hugs you. . . . It feels good to have Jesus hug you and be made to feel so welcome, doesn't it? . . . Listen, Jesus is beginning his story:

"Once upon a time there was a very rich man who owned a large farm. He had two sons who helped him on the farm. One day one of his sons came to him and told him that he wanted to take all the money that his father was going to give him when he was older and leave home. He told his father that he was tired of being good and working around the farm all day. He wanted to go to the big city and have a lot of fun. So the father gave his son all the money he had saved for him and sadly watched his son leave for the big city.

The son rented a large, beautiful apartment, made many friends and had a wonderful time doing just what he wanted to do. However, one day he discovered he no longer had any money . . . for he had spent it all. When his friends found this out they left him, and the apartment manager made him leave his beautiful apartment. The son had no place to live, no friends, and no money. He was all alone and forced to find a job. A farmer hired him to take care of his pigs. It was very hard for him to do this, for he did not like to be around pigs.

One day the son was so tired, hungry, and dirty that he decided to quit his job and go home to his father. He would tell his father he was sorry and ask him for a job on his farm where he would have good meals, a warm place to sleep, and not have to take care of pigs. Now ever since he left, his father would stand each day on a hill overlooking the road and watch for his son. And then, one day he saw his son coming down the road! He jumped for joy, clapped his hands, and ran down the road to meet his son! Oh, how happy he was! Before his son could say anything his father hugged and hugged him and told him everything was all right now that he was home. . . . He was his son once again.

When they reached home the father called all his friends and invited them to a wonderful party, for his son had returned home. When the other son came home from work and saw what was happening he was angry and told the father that he was never given a party and he was faithful and worked hard on the farm ... not like his brother who took all his money and left home. The father put his arms around his son and told him he knew this and appreciated all that the son faithfully did for him, but his brother had returned home and was sorry for what he did, and that's why they were having a party."

Jesus turns to you ... takes your hand ... looks into your eyes ... and says, "The father in my story is like my Father in heaven ... who loves you so much that He is always waiting to forgive you for anything.... Now how does that make you feel, to know that you are loved so much by my Father?"

I will give you a quiet time so that you can talk to Jesus about this.

Prayer

Jesus, I'm glad you told me the story about God's love for me and always wanting to forgive me. Help me to be sorry when I do something I'm not supposed to do and help me to try and not do it again. I love you, Jesus, and I'm glad you are my friend. Amen.

It's time to leave Jesus.... Say good-bye.... Give Jesus a hug.... You can always come back here and meet Jesus, you know, any time you want to.... Get up now and begin to walk away.... Turn and wave good-bye.... Continue to walk away.... Open your eyes and come back into the room.

Sharing

Would anyone like to share thoughts about the loving father and the two sons? What happened? Did the father forgive the son? What did the son say to the father when he returned home? Sometimes, we are selfish. What can we do when that happens?

Follow-up

Distribute colored paper cut in three-inch circles. Instruct the children to make a name badge. Explain: Your last name means that you belong to a family. Your first name reminds you that you belong to the Christian family through baptism. Just like the loving father in the story, God calls you by name and welcomes you back every time, no matter how you have failed.''

Children are invited to decorate badges with rainbows, suns, or other symbols that remind them of God's love. Children may wear their badges or hang them in a prominent place.

Closing Prayer

Gather the children near the Bible and candle.

invite the children to pray with you.

''Let us think of the times we have failed (Pause.) How have you failed? (Pause.)

Let us ask God, our Father, for His loving forgiveness. (Pause.)

Let us ask God to help us grow closer and closer to Jesus.'' (Pause.)

Pray aloud: ''Bless my family (whisper names), my friends. (Pause.)

Help each one of them to know that we have a loving Father. Amen.''

As a family, let us join hands and sing . . . pray the ''Our Father.''

Music

''God Is Our Father'' by Carey Landry from *Hi God!* (NALR)

''What Makes Love Grow?'' by Carey Landry from *Hi God!* (NALR)

The Good Samaritan

Luke 10:29–37

Who Is Our Neighbor?

Introduction

Sometimes we would rather play than help a friend, wouldn't we? ... even when that friend needs our help. . . . Have you known someone who refused to help a friend in need? (Allow time to share.) Jesus talked about just this. He told us that we must help others. . . . He told us to love our neighbor. But who is our neighbor?

One day someone asked Jesus that question and Jesus answered the question by telling a story. . . . Would you like to go to Jesus and listen to him as he tells a story about being a good neighbor? . . . Jesus is about to begin his story so let's close our eyes. . . . Take a deep breath . . . relax . . . and go to Jesus. . . .

Meditation

You are in a lovely field filled with blue and yellow and red flowers. . . . Do you see the butterflies dancing from flower to flower? . . . And listen to the songs of the birds! . . . They must be in that large shade tree just ahead of you. . . . Do you see the tree? . . . And look! . . . There is Jesus sitting under the tree! . . . There are some other children sitting around him. . . . Jesus sees you and calls you by name. . . . Run over to where Jesus is sitting. . . . He pats the ground next to him and invites you to sit down. . . . Jesus hugs you and tells you he is glad you came.

"Now let me tell you a story . . . and let's see if you can tell me who is the good neighbor." Jesus tells you. . . . "Once upon a time, there was a man traveling from Jerusalem to Jericho. . . . It was a nice day and he decided to walk. . . . He forgot that it was dangerous to walk down that road alone, for there were many robbers around. As it happened, when he was not too far out of Jerusalem, some robbers did attack him. They took all his money, and fine clothes, and they beat him up, leaving him lying half dead by the side of the road.

A priest from the temple in Jerusalem passed by, saw the poor man lying unconscious by the side of the road, and kept on walking, pretending he did not see the man. Likewise, another man of importance in the church passed by, saw the poor man, but did not stop to help him. . . . Later, another man passed by. . . . Now this man was a Samaritan and anyone from Samaria was considered a terrible sinner by the Jews; therefore, no Jew was allowed to even talk to a Samaritan. . . . Well, the Samaritan went over to the poor man, dressed his wounds, hoisted him on his horse, and took him to the nearest inn. . . . (An inn is like a motel.) He put him to bed and took care of him all night. . . . The next day the Samaritan gave some money to the innkeeper and told the innkeeper to look after the man and if there were any further expense he would pay it on his way back. . . . Jesus stops . . . turns to you . . . and asks, "Which of these three men was a good neighbor?"

I will leave you with Jesus so that you can answer the question he asked you.

Prayer

Jesus, sometimes I find it hard to keep from making fun of someone I don't like. I am sorry, Jesus. Please help me to be a good neighbor to others. I love you, Jesus. Thank you for forgiving me and understanding my problem.

It is time to leave Jesus. . . . Say good-bye. . . . Give Jesus a hug. . . . Begin to walk away. . . . Turn and

wave to Jesus once more. . . . Continue to walk away.
. . . Open your eyes and come back into the room.

Sharing

Would anyone like to share a time you have cared for others? Jesus told a story about how we must help others. What happened to the man who traveled down the road? How did the Samaritan help him? How would you answer Jesus' question, "Which of these three men was a good neighbor?"

Follow-up

Distribute (9" x 12") colored paper. Instruct the children to fold paper in half. Make a surprise card for a person. It can be a "Happy Day", "Get Well", "Thank You", or "Hello" card.

Decorate the cover of the card and print a caring message inside. When the card is finished bring, or mail, it to the person.

Some teachers make this a class project by obtaining lists of shut-ins from the parish rectory. Others have the children adopt a person or child as a "pal" to visit, call, or write all year 'round.

Prayer

The teacher gathers the children near the Bible and candle, and prays: "God, our Father, thank You for giving us Jesus. Jesus helped little children—young boys and girls, adults, and elderly. Jesus healed the sick. He touched and blessed them with His hands. Now let us place our hands on our laps upward. Let us be very quiet. Say:

(1) Be very quiet.
Feel your breath.
God gave you breath.
He gave you hands.

Think of your hands.
Think of all the hands you know: your parents,
grandparents, friends. . . .

Remember the many hands that held you. Think of all the things you made with your hands.

Remember a time when you couldn't write.

(2) Think about how often your hands helped others.

Think about how often you folded your hands in prayer.

Think of the times you waved "hello" or "good-bye".

Think now what you can do today to help someone.

(3) Now let's receive a handshake from the person beside us.

Let us reach out to be at peace and to care for each other.

Music

"This Little Light of Mine" from *Reader's Digest, Focus on Music*

The Rich Young Man

Matthew 19:16–30; Mark 10:17–31; Luke 18:18–30

Sharing with Others

Introduction

Do you have a favorite toy . . . something that is very special to you? Did your mother or your father or someone else ever ask you to share it with someone? How did you feel about that? Was it hard to do? Do you think Jesus wants us to share with others? . . . Why?

Let's be with Jesus when he talks about sharing to a very rich young boy. The boy wanted to know how he could follow Jesus.

Close your eyes. . . . Take a deep breath . . . and relax. . . .

Meditation

You are walking with Jesus and his disciples. . . . It is very warm out but there are many shade trees along the way. . . . Feel how cool it is when you walk in the shade. . . . The birds enjoy the shade trees too. . . . Do you hear them singing? . . . There is a butterfly on that red flower under the tree. . . . Do you see it? . . . Listen, someone is calling Jesus! . . . Turn around and see who it is. . . . A young boy is running toward you. . . . He has very nice clothes on, don't you think? . . . He must be very rich to have such nice clothes. . . . Stop and wait for the boy to catch up with you. . . . He

45

doesn't look at you but only at Jesus. . . . He is out of breath from running so fast . . . but that doesn't stop him from asking Jesus a question. . . . Listen to his question. . . . "Jesus, what can I do to go to heaven?"

Jesus sits down and smiles at the boy. . . . "Well," he tells him, "Keep my commandments." . . . "I do, I do!" the boy says. "I always try to obey my parents and try to be good." . . . Jesus smiles at him and says, "If you really want to follow what I teach then there is one more thing you need to do." . . . Notice how excited the boy is. . . . "What is that?" he asks Jesus. . . . "You must learn to share your things with others, especially with those who do not have as much as you have," Jesus tells him. . . . The boy stares at Jesus. . . . He looks unhappy, doesn't he? . . . Look, he is turning away from Jesus! . . . He doesn't even say "thank you." He just leaves. . . . Isn't that too bad? . . . I wonder if he knows that Jesus loves him. . . . Do you think he knows?

Jesus watches the rich boy leave. . . . Jesus looks sad, doesn't he? . . . He sighs and turns to you. . . . "I know it is hard to give up things, he tells you . . . and he places his arm around your shoulders and hugs you. . . . "Come, let us walk together. I want to ask you something." . . . Isn't it wonderful to be walking with Jesus? . . . He asks you a question, "Do you think what I asked that young boy to do is important to do?" . . . Jesus stops . . . turns and looks into your eyes. . . . "Would you be willing to share with others . . . especially my poor people?" he asks. . . . What would you like to tell Jesus?

I will give you a quiet time so that you can be alone with Jesus and talk to him.

Prayer

Jesus, sometimes it is very hard for me to share my favorite things with someone else. I will try hard to be generous like you want me to be. I know you will help me. I love you, Jesus, and am glad you are my friend. Amen.

It is time to leave Jesus. . . . Tell him good-bye. . . . Give him a nice, big hug. . . . Walk away. . . . Come back into the room and open your eyes.

Sharing

Would anyone like to share thoughts about the story? What did the rich young boy ask Jesus? What was Jesus' answer? Why did the rich young boy feel unhappy about what Jesus said? Are you willing to share some of your things with others?

Follow-up

Prepare beforehand magazine pictures: people, food, toys, money, houses, and such. Have paste, scissors, poster board, and markers ready.

Divide the children into groups of three or four. Explain to the children that they are going to make a "Sharing Collage".

Instruct the groups to share scissors, pictures, and paste. Have them cut out pictures and paste in an overlapping way on the poster board background. What goes on the sign? They then print a sign to be added to the collage. On the other side of the "Sharing Collage" each child prints his/her name. Orally they tell what picture they chose and why they chose it. The "Sharing Collages" can decorate bulletin boards, or be used during a Liturgy Celebration.

Prayer

Gather the children together around the Bible and candle. Pick up the Bible reverently and pray from Psalm 106:1.

"Thank you, Lord. How good You are: Your love goes on forever." Lower the Bible. Then, pray the closing prayer for the children.

"We know the Lord Jesus is with us. He invites us to follow His way of love. Let us pray to Jesus for help.

Help us to love You, Jesus.

Help us to share our food and money.

Help us to share our toys and time.

Forgive us for the times we are selfish.

Take all of us, dear Jesus. Help us to follow Your way of love always. We ask this through you, Jesus, our Lord. Amen.''

Sing a song.

Music

"Oh, How I Love Jesus!" by Carey Landry from *Hi God!* (NALR)

The Wicked Servant

Matthew 18:23–35

Forgiving Others

Introduction

Did you ever have someone say, or do, something to hurt you? What did you want to do when that happened? How did you feel? It is hard to forgive that person, isn't it? Peter must have been having a hard time forgiving someone because he asked Jesus how many times one should forgive another person . . . seven times? . . . Jesus told Peter that he should *always* forgive another person. He tells a story to give Peter an example of forgiveness. Let's go and be with Jesus and listen to his story.

Close your eyes. . . . Take a deep breath . . . and relax. . . .

Meditation

You are standing on some soft green grass under a large tree . . . and, if you look around, you will see that there are other children your age sitting under the tree. . . . Jesus' disciples are also there. . . . See, there is Peter sitting near Jesus. . . . He's the one who asked Jesus about forgiving others. . . . Jesus sees you and smiles. . . . He calls your name. . . . Look, he is patting the ground next to him. . . . He wants you to sit there. . . . "I've been waiting for you," Jesus tells you. "Come sit by me . . . I'm going to tell everyone a story about forgiving others." . . . Run over and sit next to Jesus. . . . He puts his arm around you and gives you a quick hug of welcome. . . . It's good to be here with Jesus and his friends, isn't it? . . . Listen, Jesus is beginning to tell his story. . . .

"Once upon a time . . . a long time ago . . . there was a great king who decided to collect all the money owed him by his servants. . . . Now there was one servant who had borrowed a great deal of money from the king and he was the first one the king decided to see. . . . The servant came trembling before the king. . . . 'Pay back all the money you owe me,' the king demanded. The servant shook from head to foot for he did not have the money. 'I do not have the money,' he mumbled to the king, for he was afraid to speak out. 'What?' said the king, 'I can't hear you. Speak up.' . . . And so the servant said in a louder voice, 'Sir, I do not have the money.' . . . The king became very angry. . . . he turned to his guards and ordered, 'Sell this servant and his entire family into slavery! . . . At least I'll get back some of the money he owes me.' . . . The guards came up to the servant. . . . But before they could take hold of him the servant fell to his knees and began to plead with the king for mercy. . . . 'I promise to pay everything I owe you, if only you will give me time,' he cried.

Now the king was actually a very kind person and when he saw his servant crying and pleading he forgave him. Not only did he forgive him but he erased all his debts and the servant did not have to pay back anything! . . . He left the king happy and singing. Now on his way home he met a fellow servant who happened· to owe him some money . . . not very much at all. . . . He stopped the servant and demanded that he pay back what he owed. . . . The fellow servant pleaded for time to pay him back. . . . However, the wicked servant would not listen to his pleadings and had him put in jail until he paid back what he owed.

The king's other servants heard what had happened and were very upset. . . . They went to the king and told him what the wicked servant had done. . . . The king was shocked . . . then very angry. . . . He had the wicked servant brought before him. . . . 'How wicked you are,' the king said, 'I cancelled your debts when you begged me for mercy. Were you not to follow my example and also forgive your fellow servant his debts? . . . Before the wicked servant could say anything the king had his guards throw him in jail until all his debts were paid.''

Jesus looks at Peter. . . . "So you must do the same, Peter. Just as my Father has forgiven you, you must also forgive others.'' . . . Jesus turns to you, places his arm around your shoulders, looks into your eyes and asks, ''Are there times when it is hard for you to forgive someone? . . . Why don't we talk about it, for I want to help you.''

I will give you a quiet time to talk to Jesus.

Prayer

Jesus, thank you for always forgiving me. Help me to forgive others, especially when I find it hard. I love you, Jesus, and am glad that you love me and are my friend. Amen.

It is time to leave. . . . Say good-bye to Jesus and his friends. . . . You can always go back and continue your conversation with Jesus. . . . Begin to walk away. . . . Turn and wave good-bye. . . . Open your eyes and come back into the room.

Sharing

From what Jesus said to Peter, how many times must we forgive? The rich king forgave his servant's debts. But, what did that same servant do to his fellow servant? By this story, Jesus tells us—no matter how hard it is, we should forgive. Jesus loves us and forgives us.

Follow-up

Make a Bible bookmark. Let it be a reminder that we are to forgive from the heart. Place it in your Bible.

Cut three lengths of yarn, two of the same color and one of a different color, about a foot long. Line

up the pieces of yarn and tie them together into a knot about one inch from one end.

Braid by folding A over B and then C over A. Continue until the yarn is braided. Tie the strands into a knot again about one inch from the end.

Cut six small hearts from white paper. Write a three-word message on three hearts, one word on each heart. Write the same message, or a different one, on the other three hearts. Glue the hearts to the end of the braid.

Option: Pass out colored strips of paper (2" x 10"). Pass out 12" pieces of colored ribbon. Instruct the children to print on one card "I Forgive", then design the card. Place the colored ribbon on the back center of the card. Glue the second card on back. This way the colored ribbon extends out on each end. Have the children keep the bookmarks in their Bibles.

Prayer

Gather the children near the Bible and candle. Open the Bible to Matthew 18:21–22. Pray: "Listen to the Word of God." (Raise Bible.)

"Then Peter went up to Jesus and said, 'Lord, how often must I forgive my brother if he wrongs me? As often as seven times?' Jesus answered, 'Not seven, I tell you, but seventy-seven times.' "

Place the Bible down reverently.

Pray silently in your hearts for forgiveness. Ask God to help you to forgive, even when it hurts. Tell God you are sorry and will begin again. (Pause.)

Close with a song.

Music

"Peace Is Flowing Like a River" by Carey Landry from *Hi God! 2* (NALR)

"Oh, How I Love Jesus!" by Carey Landry from *Hi God!* (NALR)

Mary and Martha

Luke 10:38–42

Friendship

Introduction

Jesus had some very close friends besides the disciples. Their names were Mary and Martha. Do you have close friends . . . someone you like to be with? Sometimes, when Jesus wanted to relax or when he was troubled, he would go to Mary and Martha's house, just to be with them. Do you ever go to your friend's house when you have a problem? Do you talk to your friend about your problem—or do you just hang around your friend's house just to be close to him or her? It's good to have a special friend, isn't it? Especially when you need one, like Jesus did.

Jesus was on his way to Jerusalem even though he knew that some people there wanted him arrested. His disciples were telling him it was too dangerous to go there. They were trying to talk him out of it. But Jesus knew that his heavenly Father wanted him to go there for a reason. Therefore, Jesus wanted to go. However, he needed his special friends at this time, just to be with them. And so, on his way to Jerusalem, he stopped by Mary and Martha's house. You are Jesus' special friend, aren't you? Would you like to be there with him? All right. . . . Close your eyes. . . . Take a deep breath . . . and relax. . . .

55

Meditation

You are standing in front of Mary and Martha's house. . . . It's a small house with many flowers in the yard. . . . Aren't they beautiful flowers, especially the red ones? . . . Walk up to the door and knock. . . . Mary opens the door. . . . She recognizes you and takes your hand. . . . "I'm so glad you came," she whispers. "Jesus is here with his disciples. . . . He seems troubled. . . . He needs his friends with him now." . . . Mary leads you into the house. . . . Martha hurries out of the kitchen and welcomes you . . . but excuses herself right away and rushes back into the kitchen. . . . She must be very busy, don't you think? . . . Mary leads you to Jesus. . . . Jesus looks very serious, doesn't he?

Jesus sees you . . . smiles . . . calls you by name and opens up his arms. . . . Run into Jesus' arms. Let him give you a good hug. . . . Doesn't it feel good to be hugged by Jesus? . . . "I'm glad you are here," he tells you. . . . "Come, sit by me." . . . Mary sits by Jesus, too. . . . The disciples welcome you. . . . John comes over and sits with you. . . . "It's good to see you again," he tells you. "We are trying to stop Jesus from going to Jerusalem. Maybe you can help us talk him out of it." . . . Peter is about to say something but Martha rushes in from the kitchen . . . stands in front of Jesus and points to Mary. . . . "Jesus, will you tell Mary to come and help me in the kitchen?" . . . Jesus looks at Martha. . . . "Martha, don't go to all the trouble of cooking a big meal," he tells her. . . . "Come and be with me like Mary and my friend here." He places his hand on your shoulder . . . smiles at you and whispers your name. . . . "All I want right now is to just be with my friends." . . . Martha looks at Jesus . . . frowns . . . turns and rushes back into the kitchen muttering something about people "still have to eat." . . . Jesus watches Martha leave. . . . He sighs. . . .

Cuddle up closer to Jesus. . . . Let him know that you want to comfort him. . . . Jesus smiles and hugs you. . . . "I'm glad you understand that all I need is for you to be with me now," Jesus tells you. . . . He takes your hand and asks you. . . . "Did you ever need a friend like I need one now?" . . . What would you like to say to Jesus? . . . I'll give you a quiet time so that you and Jesus can talk together.

Prayer

Jesus, I'm glad we are friends and I want everybody to know that you are my good friend. . . . Help me, Jesus, to be a good friend to you and to others. And, Jesus, help me to learn what it means to be a friend. I love you, Jesus. Amen.

It is time to leave. Say good-bye to Jesus. . . . Get up and begin to leave Mary and Martha's house. . . . Turn and wave good-bye once more. . . . Walk out of the door. . . . Open your eyes and come back into the room.

Sharing

How do you know that Jesus cared about Mary and Martha? What was the "important thing" that Mary did? How can listening to someone make a person feel welcome? Do you enjoy it when your friends listen to you?

Follow-up

Gather the children around you and tell the children that they are going to listen to one another. Invite the children to open their library books. Take turns listening. When the children have had a turn reading a few lines, ask the children to think about how they felt having someone listen while they read. Share how it feels to have someone listen. Was it fun reading? Was it fun listening?

Prayer

Gather around the Bible and candle.

Teacher says:

"Close your eyes and think of times that you can listen better . . . times with a friend, times at school, time at home."

Invite the children to pray:

"Dear Jesus,

Listen to each of us pray "thank you" for being our friend, and "thank you" for: (Invite the children to spontaneous prayer.)

We can never stop thanking you, Jesus. Help us always to listen. We love You, Jesus. We are sorry for the times we did not listen to You and others. Bless each one of us and help us grow closer to You and one another. Amen."

Close with a song.

Music

"Listen, Listen" by Brenda Bischoff and Carey Landry from *Hi God!* (NALR)

"Hi God!" by Carey Landry from *Hi God!* (NALR)

Jesus Washes the Feet
of His Disciples

John 13:1–17

Helping Others

Introduction

There are many ways we can help others. Can you think of ways to help someone? Do you think that it is important to help others? Jesus wants us to help other people, doesn't he? In fact, he was always helping others, especially those people whom no one else liked or wanted to be near. On the night before he died, Jesus was trying for the last time to teach this to his friends, the disciples. Let's go and be with Jesus at this time, because we are also his friends. . . .

Close your eyes. . . . Take a deep breath . . . and relax. . . .

Meditation

It is the night that Jesus is going to be arrested. Jesus knows this and is very sad. You are with Jesus and his disciples, waiting to eat the Passover meal. . . . Jesus has you sitting next to him. . . . John is sitting next to you. . . . Smell the aroma of food that fills the room. . . . It makes your mouth water, doesn't it? . . . The room is not very bright for it is lighted by lanterns . . . the kind people use when they go camping. . . . See how the flames from the lanterns cast dancing shadows on the walls and ceiling? . . . If you look to the back of the room you will see women preparing the meal. . . . They aren't talking much. . . . It doesn't seem to be a happy time, does it? . . .

Jesus puts his hand on your shoulder and says your name. . . . "Will you get me a basin, a towel, and a pitcher of water? . . . The women will give these to you." . . . One of the women overhears Jesus tell you this. . . . She smiles at you and points to a table in the corner of the room. . . . Go over to the table and get the basin, towel, and pitcher of water and bring it to Jesus. . . . Jesus thanks you and lets you hold the basin. . . . "I'm going to wash the feet of the disciples and your feet too," Jesus tells you. "Follow me around the room," he says. . . . Put the basin by the feet of John and watch Jesus as he washes and dries John's feet. Peter is the only one who argues with Jesus because he doesn't want Jesus to wash his feet. . . . Jesus looks up at Peter and tells him that it is important for him to do this. . . . You are glad when Peter lets Jesus wash his feet. . . . The other disciples are glad, too. Jesus takes the basin from you . . . and has you sit down so he can wash your feet. . . . Jesus looks at you . . . pats your hand. . . . "Do you know why I am doing this?" he asks you. . . . "I am trying to teach all my friends how important it is to help others." Jesus gently washes your feet. . . . Feel the cool water on your feet and Jesus' strong hands as he holds your feet. . . . Now Jesus dries your feet. . . . Feel the soft towel. . . . Watch Jesus. . . . See the love he has for you as he washes and dries your feet. . . . How do you feel having Jesus wash your feet?

Jesus leans back and looks up into your eyes. . . . "Will you serve others as I have just served you?" Jesus smiles . . . leans forward and says . . . "Will you follow my example and help others?" . . . Jesus waits for your answer.

What would you like to say to Jesus? I will give you a quiet time so that you can answer Jesus' question and talk to him. . . .

Prayer

Jesus, I want to help other people just like you taught me when you washed my feet. . . . Sometimes,

I might be afraid to offer to help someone. Sometimes maybe I'd rather be playing with my friends. You are my friend, Jesus, and I know that you will help me to do good to others. I love you, Jesus, my friend. Amen.

It is time to leave Jesus. . . . Say good-bye. . . . Begin to walk away. . . . Turn and wave good-bye. . . . Continue to walk away. . . . Open your eyes and come back into the room.

Sharing

Why were Jesus and His disciples together? What did Jesus do before eating? Who didn't want his feet washed? What was Jesus trying to teach us? Would anyone like to share a time when you helped someone? Who was it? What did you do?

Follow-up

Pass out xeroxed or dittoed footprint papers. On the bottom of the paper have words and phrases of ways we can help. (1) Set the table. (2) Share toys. (3) Obey. (4) Visit or send a card to the sick. (5) Clean up my room. (6) Go to the store. (7) Help a friend.

Direct the children to print their names on the heel, and then circle a way they choose to help. Put the number of the chosen circled phrase on the footprint. The footprint papers can be taken home and displayed. The teacher can collect footprints, make a mural, or bulletin board. Together, choose a caption.

Some may choose to trace the footprint on colored paper and cut it out. In this case, the phrases and words are printed on newsprint or on the board.

Prayer

Gather the children near the Bible and candle. Remind the children that whenever we gather in Jesus' name, He is with us. (Pause.) Say: Today, Jesus tells us, "Serve the Lord Jesus with gladness." (Pause.)

Think now of your footprint and what way you promised to help. Let us stand and bless each other as we go out to serve and help. (All raise hands in blessing.)

Pray:

"Bless us, Lord Jesus. Help us to serve You better every day. We ask this in the (sign of cross) name of the Father, and of the Son, and of the Holy Spirit. Amen."

Close with song.

Music

"Come Along with Me to Jesus," by Carey Landry from *Hi God! 2* (NALR)

"Come and Go With Me" (author unknown) from *Hi God! 2* (NALR)

The Last Supper

Mark 14:22–25; Luke 22:17–20;
Matthew 26:26–29

Jesus' Love for Us

Introduction

When you love someone very much, do you always want to be with that person? What are some of the reasons you give so that you can be together? Can you always be with that person?

Jesus loved us so much that he wanted to be with us always, and he found a way to do this. For, at the Last Supper, Jesus did something very special for us. What do you suppose that was? Let's be with Jesus and his friends at his last supper on earth when he does something very special just for us. Close your eyes.... Take a deep breath ... and relax....

Meditation

You are in a room where Jesus and his disciples are eating supper.... Look around the room.... There are no electric lights, are there? ... There are just candles, attached to holders on the walls.... See how their flames make dancing shadows on the walls and ceiling? ... The disciples see you.... Peter gets up and puts his arm around your shoulders ... calls you by name ... and welcomes you.... "Come, join us." The other disciples smile and invite you to have supper with them.... It's nice to be made to feel welcome, isn't it? ... Someone else calls you by name. . . . Look over there at the head of the table. . . . It is Jesus. . . . "I'm glad you have come to join us," Jesus tells you. . . . "Come and sit down by me." . . . Run over and sit next to Jesus. . . . He gives you a nice big hug. . . . Doesn't it feel good to be here next to Jesus?

Jesus now turns from you and takes a piece of bread off the large plate in front of him. . . . It doesn't look like regular bread. . . . It looks more like pita bread, doesn't it? . . . He tears off a piece . . . turns to you and gives you the piece of bread. . . . Jesus tells you, "Take this and eat it, for this is my body." . . . Feel Jesus' hand touch yours as he gives you the bread. . . . He is looking into your eyes with love. . . . Take the piece of bread and eat it. . . . It tastes a little like pita bread, doesn't it? . . . Jesus passes the bread to the others. . . . Everyone is now eating the bread. . . . No one is talking. . . . They all look very serious because they are afraid that Jesus will be arrested tonight. . . . Jesus now takes his cup of wine and prays a blessing over it . . . gives the cup to you . . . and says, "This is my blood to be poured out for many." . . . Take the cup from Jesus. . . . Taste the wine. . . . It tastes like grape juice, doesn't it? . . . Pass the cup of wine to John. . . . Jesus touches your hand. . . . See his love for you in his eyes. . . . He softly speaks your name . . . and says, "I love you so much that I want to be with you always. . . . That is why I have done this. . . . Do you love me?" . . . What would you like to say to Jesus? . . . I'll give you a quiet time so that you and Jesus can talk together.

Prayer

Thank you, Jesus, for loving me so much. I want to be with you always so I am glad that you gave yourself to me in this special way—because we can now be together all the time. I love you very much, Jesus. You are my best friend. Amen.

It is time to leave. . . . Say good-bye to Jesus and the disciples. . . . Get up and begin to walk out of the room. . . . Turn and wave goodbye to Jesus once more. . . . Walk out of the room. . . . Open your eyes and come back into the room.

Sharing

Think of a time you shared food with your family and friends. Why was it so special? Jesus loved us so much that He wanted to be with us always. What did Jesus share with His friends the night before He died? What does Jesus ask us to do in memory of Him?

Follow-up

Give the children a ditto sheet with a table altar on it. Beforehand, print the directions at the bottom of the page. Go over directions aloud with the children.

Put candles at the side of the altar. Draw a large book on the altar. Draw a priest at the altar. Draw people around the altar. Draw pitchers to hold water and wine. Draw a plate to hold the host. Draw a chalice (cup). Display the children's pictures.

Prayer

Gather the children near the Bible and candle. Have Bible opened to 1 Corinthians 11:23–25. Raise the Bible reverently and pray.

". . . the Lord Jesus, on the night He was betrayed took a piece of bread, gave thanks to God, broke it, and said: 'This is My body, which is for you. Do this in memory of Me.' In the same way, after the supper He took the cup and said, 'This cup is God's new covenant, sealed with My blood. Whenever you drink it, do so in memory of Me.' "

"This is the Word of the Lord."

Lower Bible.

All pray: "Amen," and close with song.

Music

"We Come to Your Table," by Carey Landry from *Hi God! 2* (NALR)

"Come, Lord Jesus," by Carey Landry from *Hi God 2* (NALR)

The Vine and Branches

John 15:1–8

We Need Jesus as Our Friend
Jesus Wants to Be Our Best Friend

Introduction

Isn't it wonderful to have a best friend? Does anyone here have a best friend? Did you become best friends right away, or did it take a little while for you to get to know each other? Did anyone ever have a best friend move far away? How did you feel? Did you want to keep that person as your friend? What would you have to do to keep that person as your friend? What would happen if you did not keep in touch with your friend?

This happened to Jesus. . . . His friends, the disciples, would not be seeing him any more and he wanted to talk about this with them. . . .

Let's go to Jesus and be with him as he talks to his close friends. . . . Close your eyes. . . . Take a deep breath . . . and relax. . . .

Meditation

Jesus and his disciples have just finished supper. . . . It was the Passover meal that all Jews were celebrating, and it is Jesus' last supper with his disciples. . . . He knows that he is going to be arrested tonight and will most likely die on the cross tomorrow. . . . He is very sad . . . and so are his disciples . . . and so are you, for you are with them. . . .

67

Look around the room.... Watch Jesus get up from the table.... He sighs.... He seems sad, doesn't he? . . . Look at the disciples.... They don't seem happy either.... They all look worried.... Peter sees you, walks over to you, and says, "It's dangerous for Jesus to be in Jerusalem, for some people want him arrested and put out of the way."

Jesus walks up to you ... places his arm around your shoulders and says, "I'm glad you have come. I need my friends with me now." Jesus leads you outside.... The disciples follow.... No one is talking.... Everyone seems worried.... Notice that the moon is very bright and, although it is night, it doesn't seem dark.... And listen! ... It all seems so quiet outside. . . . That's because all the Jews are home celebrating the Passover meal....

Jesus stops and looks at a grapevine by the house. ... He points to the large, twisted vine.... "See that vine? ... I am like that vine ... and you are like the branches coming from the vine." Jesus looks at you. . . . He wants you to understand what he is trying to tell you.... "What would happen if one of these branches broke off from the vine?" ... Jesus waits for you to answer.... (Allow the children to answer out loud if you wish.) Jesus nods his head.... "Yes, the branch would shrivel and die because it no longer gets food from the vine."

Jesus stoops down and places his arms around you ... looks into your eyes and tells you ... "That's why it is so important for you to stay close to me and talk to me, even though you won't see me. Because friendships also need to be fed just like this branch." Jesus picks a bunch of delicious purple grapes from the branch and invites you to share them with him. . . . Taste and see how sweet and delicious the grapes are.... It's good to be here with Jesus, isn't it? ... "It's a very happy grape vine, isn't it?" Jesus says.

Jesus begins to walk down the street.... He sighs . . . stops ... looks at you and asks, "Will you let me be your best friend?"

I will give you quiet time so that you can answer Jesus.

Prayer

Jesus, I promise to come and talk to you often. . . . Even though I don't see you, I know you are with me . . . because you told me, and you are my best friend. And that's what friends are for, to be with each other and to share. I love you, Jesus. Amen.

It's time to leave. . . . Say good-bye to Jesus for now. . . . You can always return. . . . Begin to walk away. . . . Turn and wave good-bye once more. . . . Open your eyes and come back into the room.

Sharing

How could you keep in touch with your friend if he/she moved away? Why did Jesus tell the story of the vine and the branches? What do you suppose Jesus wanted the apostles to do when they no longer could see Him?

Follow-up

Have ready a poster board, a brown paper cut-out vine, strips of brown paper branches, and purple circles for grapes.

Pass out the cut-out vine and the brown strips of paper; then, give each child a purple-circle grape.

Directions for poster making:

First, a child prints "Jesus" on the vine and glues it to the poster board.

Then, each child with a brown branch, glues it to the vine.

Next, each child initials his/her grape and glues it on (forming a cluster of grapes).

Finally, the teacher adds caption, "Jesus is the Vine. . . . We are the Branches."

An alternative would be to have children use markers to draw the vine, branches, and clusters of

grapes. Add caption "Jesus is the Vine. . . . We are the Branches."

Prayer

Gather the children around the Bible and candle. Place poster nearby. **Teacher prays:**

Jesus, thank You for Your friendship.

You feed us in many ways. You come to us especially in the Eucharist.

Help us grow. We know You are with us. We love You, Jesus.

Thank You for our family and friends. (Invite spontaneous thanksgiving prayers.) Close with song.

Music

"Sing a Simple Song" by Carey Landry from *Hi God! 2* (NALR)

"Thank You, Lord" by Carey Landry from *Hi God!* (NALR)

Peter Denies He Knows Jesus

Luke 22:54–62; John 18:15–27; Mark 14:66–72; Matthew 17:69–75

Honesty and Faithfulness

Introduction

Sometimes it is hard to tell the truth, isn't it? Especially when we are afraid that we might be punished. And maybe you know someone who was even afraid to admit to others that he or she had a certain person as a friend. Can you give me some reasons why anyone would be afraid to admit that? I wonder how that person would feel after denying a friendship with another person. Would it have been better to be honest in the first place? Why? Jesus' friend, Peter, became so afraid when Jesus was arrested that he denied he knew Jesus when he was asked. I wonder how Peter felt when he did that? . . . Let's go and be with Peter at this time, shall we?

Close your eyes. . . . Take a deep breath . . . and relax. . . .

Meditation

It is nighttime. . . . You are in a dusty courtyard outside the building where Jesus has been taken after being arrested. . . . It is cold outside. . . . But if you look straight ahead you will see that there is a bonfire in the middle of the courtyard. . . . Soldiers and servants are standing around the fire to keep warm. . . . You are with Peter. . . . He touches your shoulder and points toward the bonfire. . . . "We better stand by the fire to keep warm," he tells you. . . . "No telling how long they will be keeping Jesus in there." . . . He glances toward the building and frowns. . . . It's terrible to know that Jesus is arrested, isn't it? . . .

Sit by the fire with Peter. . . . Are you beginning to feel warm? . . . A woman servant comes up and looks at Peter. . . . "This man is one of Jesus' friends," she tells the others by the fire. . . . Peter looks at the woman and says, "Woman, I don't even know him." . . . How do you feel when Peter says that? . . . Peter doesn't look at you. . . . He just stares at the fire. . . . He probably feels bad about what he just did. . . . Another servant comes up to Peter . . . nods his head and says to him, "You are one of Jesus' followers." . . . Notice that the soldiers have stopped talking and are watching Peter. . . . "No, I'm not!" Peter tells him. . . . The soldiers turn away and continue talking to each other. . . . Peter's shoulders sag. . . . He sighs and stares into the fire. . . . Later, another man comes up to Peter, stares at him, and then says to the people around the fires, "This man was certainly with Jesus for he is a Galilean." . . . Peter jumps up . . . looks at the man and says, "My friend, I do not know what you are talking about."

Listen. . . . There is a commotion by the building. . . . Guards have opened the door and are leading Jesus across the courtyard. . . . Jesus looks so tired, doesn't he? . . . and his hands are tied! . . . It is all very sad, isn't it? . . . Jesus looks into Peter's eyes as he passes. . . . Jesus looks into your eyes. . . . How does this make you feel? . . . A rooster crows. . . . A soldier shoves Jesus ahead, "Come on. Get going!" he tells Jesus . . . and Jesus is led away. . . . There is the sound of someone crying. . . . Turn and see Peter crying. . . . He is leaning up against a wall. . . . His arm covers his eyes. . . . His body is shaking from crying. . . . Go over and place your hand on Peter's arm to let him know you are with him. "I was warned by Jesus that I would do this," Peter chokes out. . . . His arm still covers his eyes. . . . "But I was so afraid. . . . If those people saw that I knew Jesus they might have had me arrested too." Peter continues to cry as he looks at you helplessly. . . . What would you like to say to

Peter? . . . I'll give you some quiet time so you and Peter can talk about what happened.

Prayer

Peter, I know that you love Jesus. I know you didn't want to deny him. . . . I have found it hard to be honest sometimes too because I become afraid just like you. I'm so glad that Jesus loves us so much that he is ready to forgive us . . . no matter what we have done! Amen.

It is time to leave Peter. . . . Say good-bye. . . . Give Peter a big hug. . . . Start walking away. . . . Turn and wave good-bye once more. . . . Open your eyes and come back into the room.

Sharing

How do you think Peter felt about himself after he denied that he knew Jesus? Why did he deny that he knew Jesus? Would it have taken courage to admit the truth? Why? In your own life, does it sometimes take courage to admit the truth about something? Why?

Follow-up

What are some situations in which we might be tempted to be dishonest? List on the board. Together with the children, discuss how the situations could be solved. Print on the board the responses. Invite the children to choose one situation. Act out the situation. (This is an excellent opportunity to use puppets.) One person will be caught "in the act of" doing something wrong (fighting, taking something that doesn't belong to him/her, lying, gossiping about a friend). The other person will be the one who catches him "in the act." The one caught will start excusing himself/herself and then eventually tell the truth.

An alternative would be to draw a picture of the situation. Fold paper in two. On one side of the paper show fighting, lying, and such. On the other side, show how the problem is solved. Share drawings with one another.

Prayer

Gather around the Bible and candle. The teacher prays: "When we fail, even when we are not caught, we need to be honest with ourselves. We need to be honest with others. Sometimes, that is very hard, but Jesus is always there to forgive. Jesus has given us the Sacrament of Reconciliation. Our priest forgives in Jesus' name and we promise to be more honest and faithful in the future." Close the session by a simple Act of Contrition and sing a song.

Music

"Jesus, Jesus" and "Pardon Your People" from *Young People's Glory and Praise* (NALR)

"Peace Time" by Carey Landry from *Hi God!* (NALR)

Jesus Carries His Cross

Matthew 27:32; Mark 15:21;
Luke 23:26–32

Loving Your Neighbor

Introduction

Jesus told us to love everybody when he said that we should love our neighbor. There are special times when someone needs our love and understanding. Can you tell me when this would be? Have you ever been hurt? Maybe you fell, or maybe you just didn't feel good inside . . . or were sad. Was a friend there to help you? How did your friend help you? Were you glad your friend was there? Sometimes there isn't much a person can do but just be with a friend when the friend is hurting. Is this important?

Once Jesus was hurting very much. He had been arrested, put in jail, beaten up by the soldiers, and made to carry his cross to a place where the soldiers were going to crucify him. . . . This was happening to Jesus because he loved us so much. . . . Let's go and be with our friend, Jesus. . . . Close your eyes. . . . Take a deep breath . . . and relax. . . .

Meditation

There is a large crowd standing along a narrow street waiting for Jesus to come by. He is on his way to be crucified. . . . It is a very sad time, isn't it? . . . You are standing at the edge of the crowd with friends of Jesus. . . . Some of his friends have tears in their eyes. . . . If you listen, you will hear people talking to each other about Jesus. . . . Someone in back of you is saying, "He never did anybody any harm. . . . Why are they doing this to him?" . . . One of Jesus' friends places his hand on your shoulders and says, "I wish there were something we could do for Jesus." . . . He is about to say something more . . . but the crowd begins to whisper loudly. . . . "He's coming. . . . Jesus is coming!" . . . Look up the street. . . . Do you see Jesus coming down the street? . . . He is carrying a heavy cross. . . . See the soldiers with him? . . . Look, Jesus is falling! . . . Everyone around you begins to cry out, "Someone help him!" . . . A soldier grabs a man out of the crowd and forces him to help Jesus carry his heavy cross . . . while another soldier helps Jesus up. . . . One of Jesus' friends runs out of the crowd and tries to help Jesus but the soldier pushes him back. . . .

Jesus is now in front of you. . . . He falls again! . . . What can you do? . . . What do you want to do for your friend, Jesus? . . . Is there something you want to tell him? . . . I will give you a quiet time so that you can be with Jesus. . . .

Prayer

Jesus, I wanted to help you so much . . . to stop you from being hurt. . . . When you were on earth you taught us that if we help others who are hurting, we are helping you because you love everybody and we are all your Father's children. I am glad I know this, because now I know how I can help you. I love you, Jesus. Amen.

It is time to leave. . . . It might be a little hard to say good-bye . . . but Jesus understands. . . . Tell Jesus you love Him. . . . Turn and walk away. . . . Open your eyes and come back into the room.

Sharing

Would anyone like to share a time when you hurt? What happened? Was a friend there to help you? Why was this a hard time for Jesus? Did anyone come and help Jesus when He fell carrying His cross?

Jesus teaches us that in helping one another we are really helping Him.

Follow-up

Pass out (9" x 12") manila paper. Instruct the children to fold the paper in half. Show the children how to cut on the open side to form a half cross. Open the paper. Instruct the children to draw lines in mosaic fashion on the cross. Color in the spaces with different colors. This gives a stained glass effect. The cross reminds us of Jesus' death. The bright colors remind us that Jesus rose and is with us now. Print the child's name on the other side of the cross and hang in a special place.

Prayer

Gather the children around the Bible and candle and pray: "Sometimes, we want the easy way out. We want a good grade without working. We want a new toy without taking care of the old ones. We want a prize even if we don't run in the race. Jesus, help us to take up our daily crosses. Help us to be kind to others and help them along the way. We love You, Jesus. Today, we promise to do a kind act for someone in our family. Forgive us for the times we did not love, the times we refused to help others. Amen."

Invite the children to pray after you: "We adore You, O Christ, and we bless You, because by Your holy cross You saved us all from sin."

Close with song.

Music

"Oh, How I Love Jesus!" by Carey Landry from *Hi God!* (NALR)

"What Shall I Do?" by Carey Landry from *Hi God! 2* (NALR)

Easter Morning

Matthew 28:1–10; Mark 16:1–8;
Luke 24:1–11

Celebrate! Jesus Has Risen!

Introduction

Isn't it wonderful to have a friend like Jesus? You can go to him any time you want and you know he will always be there waiting for you. . . . And Jesus is one friend who understands everything that is deep in your heart. . . . I imagine when Jesus was on earth many, many people felt the way you do about him. Don't you think so?

Once, Jesus' close friends thought they'd lost him forever . . . and that they would never see him again. Then something wonderful happened and they were happy again. Do you know what happened? (Allow the discussion to lead to Jesus' resurrection.) Mary Magdalene was one of the first persons who saw Jesus after he rose from the dead. Let's be with Mary Magdalene when she was looking for Jesus, shall we? Close your eyes. . . . Take a deep breath . . . and relax. . . .

Meditation

You and Mary Magdalene are standing in front of the tomb where Jesus lay after he was taken down from the cross. . . . Mary is crying. . . . ''Jesus is gone!'' she tells you. . . . ''Look and see for yourself.'' The tomb is a tiny cave on the side of a rocky hill. . . . Touch and feel how rough the stones are at the entrance of the tomb. . . . Stand with Mary at the entrance and look inside. . . . Look, there are two beautiful angels!. . . . Aren't you surprised to see them? . . . They don't seem sad. They seem happy! . . . See, they are smiling at you! . . . And look at how beautiful they are! . . . Their clothes seem to be all yellows and golds and filled with light. . . . One angel looks at you and Mary and asks, "Why are you crying?" Mary doesn't seem to care if they are angels. . . . She doesn't even notice how beautiful and happy they are. . . . "Where have you put Jesus?" she asks them . . . but doesn't even wait for them to answer. . . . She suddenly grabs your hand and pulls you away. . . . "Come, let's look for Jesus in the garden," she tells you . . . and off she goes, pulling you behind her. . . . Do you wish she would stop holding your hand so tightly? . . . Just tell Mary to let go of your hand. . . . Say it nicely. . . . There, she let your hand go. . . .

See that man up ahead. . . . He seems to be watching you . . . or is he waiting for you? . . . "Let's go ask that gardener where they have laid Jesus," Mary says. . . . The gardener is smiling at both of you as though he knows you. . . . "Why are you crying?" he asks Mary. Is your heart beginning to pound from excitement? . . . Do you suppose this man isn't the gardener at all? . . . "Have you seen where they have taken Jesus?" Mary asks him. . . . The gardener smiles and calls you both by your name. . . . Feel your heart pound faster. . . . It's Jesus! . . . The gardener isn't a gardener. He is Jesus! . . . He's alive! . . . He did not leave you! . . . Aren't you happy to see Jesus? . . . He is looking at you . . . and smiling. . . . "Were you afraid that I had left you?" Jesus asks . . . Jesus reaches out and takes your hand . . . gives your hand a gentle squeeze, and leads you for a walk in the garden. . . . It is good to be alone with Jesus, isn't it? . . . Were you afraid that Jesus would leave you? . . . Why don't you and Jesus talk about this. . . . I will give you a quiet time just for you and Jesus.

Prayer

I'm so glad that you are alive and with me, Jesus. You are my friend and I want to be with you and celebrate your coming back to us. . . . I know that you will never leave me, and this makes me happy. I love you, Jesus. Amen.

It is time to leave. . . . Say good-bye to Jesus. . . . Begin to walk away. . . . Turn and wave good-bye once more. . . . Open your eyes and come back into the room.

Sharing

What happened that made Jesus' friends think they would never see Him again? Who went to the tomb on Easter morning? Why was Mary Magdalan so surprised? Why do we celebrate Easter?

Follow-up

Give each child a sheet of white paper (12" x 24"). Instruct the children to cut the paper into an egg shape. Allow time for the children to copy and print with markers, "Jesus Is Risen, Alleluia" or other Easter message.

Children can design and draw freely anything they wish that expresses the Easter message, "Jesus Is Risen." Give the egg greeting to someone special.

If there is an opportunity to dye eggs with the children, this would be a great experience of sharing and togetherness. It might be well to explain the symbolism of the egg: shell breaking open like the tomb—and chicken breaking through, new life.

Prayer

Gather the children near the Bible and candle. Holding hands, pray together after the teacher:

"Christ has died,

Christ is risen,

Christ will come again!"

All sing or pray "Alleluia."

Invite each child forward and bless his/her forehead with holy water in the sign of the cross.

Music

"Alleluia" from *Glory and Praise* (NALR)

"Rejoice in the Lord" author unknown from *Hi God!* (NALR)

On the Road to Emmaus

Luke 24:13–35

Keeping a Promise

Introduction

Do you know what it means to make a promise? Have you ever made a promise to anyone? Have you kept your promise? Has anyone ever broken a promise to you? How did you feel?

Two of Jesus' friends, one of whom was named Cleopas, felt very bad because they thought that Jesus had broken his promise to them. . . . For when he died on the cross, they thought they would never see him again. . . . And Jesus had promised that he would always love them. How could he do that now? And Jesus promised that he would never leave them, but he did when he died on the cross. . . . And it was three days since Jesus died. So, they decided to go back home . . . to their village, Emmaus. . . . They were very sad and very disappointed.

Let's join Jesus' friends and see what happens. . . . Close your eyes. . . . Take a deep breath . . . and relax.

Meditation

You are on a dirt road. . . . Feel the dust under your feet. . . . There must be birds in the trees . . . for listen to their songs! . . . It's not too hot because it's late afternoon. . . . See those two people on the road up ahead? . . . They are Jesus' friends. . . . Run and catch up with them. . . . Cleopas and his friend greet you. . . . Cleopas reaches out with his hand and takes yours. . . . Do you feel him squeeze your hand? . . . They seem very sad, don't they? . . . Their friend Jesus died, Cleopas tells you. . . . Jesus is your friend, too. . . . Do you feel sad?

A stranger comes up to you. . . . He looks at you and asks why you are so sad. . . . Tell him what happened to Jesus. . . . The stranger places his hand on your shoulder to comfort you. . . . His hand feels strong, doesn't it? . . . The stranger begins to tell you a story . . . all about God's promise . . . and, before you know it, you are in front of Cleopas' house. . . . The stranger says good-bye, but Cleopas tells him to come in and have supper. . . .

Run into the house. . . . The room is dark. . . . Open the shutters so there will be light in the room. . . . Help Cleopas put some food on the table. . . . When you are finished helping Cleopas, sit next to the stranger. . . . He smiles at you. . . . He seems happy to have you sit next to him, doesn't he? . . . The stranger takes a piece of bread . . . blesses it . . . and gives you a piece. . . . His hand touches yours . . . and suddenly, you know that the stranger is Jesus! . . . He did not leave you! . . . He is here with you . . . smiling at you. . . . He has kept his promise! . . . Jesus places his arms around you. . . . He seems to be waiting for you to talk to him. . . . What would you like to tell Jesus? . . . I'll give you a quiet time to talk to Jesus and to listen to what he wants to tell you.

Prayer

Jesus, I love you. I know you never break your promise and will always love me and be with me. Help me keep my promise to you . . . to always be your friend. Amen.

It is time to leave Jesus. . . . Say good-bye. . . . Give Jesus a hug. . . . Turn and leave the house. . . . Open your eyes and come back into the room.

Sharing

Would anyone like to share thoughts about keeping promises? What made Cleopas and his friend so sad?

Why were they going home to Emmaus? Who joined them? How did they recognize Jesus?

Follow-up

Pass out (12" x 24") paper. Illustrate how to draw a diagonal line from bottom left corner to right top corner. Children are to make the line into a road. They draw a house at the end of the road. They make a road sign, "To Emmaus". Allow children to draw freely the two friends and Jesus walking down the road and add whatever they desire to the picture.

Prayer

Gather around the Bible and candle. Place drawings nearby. **Teacher:**

Dear Jesus,

Help us to remember You are always with us.

"Jesus is with us, is risen, is with us.

Jesus is risen, is with us today.

Jesus is the lord! Jesus is the Lord!"

(Quiet moment of reflection). Listen to "Are Not Our Hearts," by Carey Landry from *Hi God!* (NALR)

Invite children to sing along with tape or record.

Music

"Are Not Our Hearts" by Carey Landry from *Hi God!* (NALR)

Index A:
Biblical Passages

Numbers given refer to the meditation number, not the page number.

Matthew 4:18–22 (5)
Matthew 8:23–27 (7)
Matthew 17:69–75 (18)
Matthew 18:1–14 (9)
Matthew 18:23–35 (13)
Matthew 19:13–15 (6)
Matthew 19:16–30 (12)
Matthew 25:14–30 (8)
Matthew 26:26–29 (16)
Matthew 27:32 (19)
Matthew 28:1–10 (20)

Mark 1:16–20 (5)
Mark 4:35–42 (7)
Mark 10:13–16 (6)
Mark 10:17–31 (12)
Mark 14:22–25 (16)
Mark 14:66–72 (18)
Mark 15:21 (19)
Mark 16:1–8 (20)

Luke 1:26–38 (1)
Luke 1:39–56 (2)
Luke 2:8–20 (3)
Luke 2:41–52 (4)
Luke 8:22–25 (7)
Luke 10:29–37 (11)
Luke 10:38–42 (14)
Luke 15:3–7 (9)
Luke 15:11–32 (10)

Luke 18:15–17 (6)
Luke 18:18–30 (12)
Luke 19:12–27 (8)
Luke 22:17–20 (16)
Luke 22:54–62 (18)
Luke 23:26–32 (19)
Luke 24:1–11 (20)
Luke 24:13–35 (21)

John 13:1–17 (15)
John 15:1–8 (17)
John 18:15–27 (18)

Index B:
Human Experience Symbols

Numbers given refer to the meditation number, not the page number.

Being (identity)—1, 4, 6, 10, 15, 21
Being faithful/honest—18
Believing—20, 21
Belonging—6, 9, 10, 17

Caring—6, 7, 9, 10, 11, 15, 16, 19, 20
Celebrating—3, 9, 10, 20, 21
Changing—5, 6, 10, 20, 21

Forgiving—9, 10, 13
Following—5, 12

Giving—8, 11, 12, 15, 16, 17, 20, 21
Growing—4

Hearing/Responding—1, 4, 5, 21

Loving—3, 9, 14, 16, 19, 20, 21

Obeying—1, 4, 5, 8

Praising—2, 3, 21

Receiving—3, 14, 21
Rejoicing—3, 9, 10, 20, 21

Risking—5, 10, 11, 19, 20

Sharing—2, 8, 12
Serving—14, 15, 19, 21

Thanking—2, 3, 10, 14, 19, 21
Trusting—1, 5, 6, 7

Welcoming—6, 10, 14, 21

Index C:
Gospel Images

Numbers given refer to the meditation number, not the page number.

The Annunciation—1
The Visitation—2
The *Magnificat*—2
Birth of Jesus—3
The Child Jesus in the Temple—4
The Call of the Disciples—5
Jesus and the Children—6
The Kingdom of Heaven—6, 12, 13, 16
The Calming of the Storm—7
The Talents—8
The Lost Sheep—9
The Prodigal Son—10
The Loving Father—10
The Good Samaritan—11
The Rich Young Ruler—12
Eternal Life—12
The Wicked Servant—13
The Judgment of God—13
Mary and Martha—14
The Washing of the Disciples' Feet—15
The Last Supper—16
The Institution of the Eucharist—16
The Vine and the Branches—17
Unity in Christ—17
Peter's Denial—18
The Scourging of Jesus—18
The Carrying of the Cross—19
Simon of Cyrene—19
The Resurrection—20
The Empty Tomb—20
Mary Magdalene—20
The Road to Emmaus—21
The Suffering Messiah—21
The Risen Lord—21
The Breaking of Bread—16, 21